YOUR PERFECT PET

LOVE YOUR DOG

Judith Heneghan

WINDMILL BOOKS
New York

Published in 2013 by Windmill Books, An Imprint of Rosen Publishing
29 East 21st Street, New York, NY 10010

Editor: Nicola Edwards
Designer: Rocket Design (East Anglia) Ltd
Picture Reasearcher: Nicola Edwards
Consultant: Anna Claxton

Picture Acknowledgements: The author and publisher would like to thank the following for allowing their pictures to be reproduced in this publication:
Cover: (main) Shutterstock/ Eric Isselée, (inset) iStock © Frans Rombout; title page P4 Shutterstock © Morgan Lane Photography; p5 RSPCA/Angela Hampton; p6 (t) Shutterstock/ Emily Sartoski; p6 iStock © Kim Gunkel; p7 Shutterstock © Tony Campbell; p8 Shutterstock/ Eric Isselée; p9 (m) Shutterstock/ Eric Isselée, (b) Shutterstock/ Petr Jilek; p10 Shutterstock © Sonya Etchison; p11 (T) RSPCA/Angela Hampton, (b) Shutterstock © Elena Elisseeva; p12 Shutterstock © tkemot; p13 (m) Shutterstock 4635022 © Mike Flippo (b) Shutterstock © Rob Kemp; p14 Shutterstock/Lisa F. Young; p15 (t) Andrew Forsyth/RSPCA, (m) RSPCA/ Angela Hampton; p16 (t) Shutterstock © AnetaPics, (b) Andrew Forsyth/RSPCA; p17 Shutterstock/ Dee Hunter; p18 (t) RSPCA/Angela Hampton, (b) Shutterstock © lightpoet; p19 istock © Monika Wisniewska; p20 (t) iStock © Loic Bernard, (b); p21 (t) Shutterstock Kachalkina Veronika, (b) Shutterstock/ Zoyaa; p22 Alamy © Bubbles Photography; p23 (t) © Jack Sullivan/Alamy, (b) iStock © Sadeugra; p24 (t) Shutterstock © ep_stock, (b) © Juniors Bildarchiv/ Alamy; p25 (t) Shutterstock/ Christian Mueller (b) Shutterstock/ Cristi Matei; p26 Shutterstock/cynoclub; p27 iStock © Brett Hillyard; p28 (t) iStock © Eileen Hart, (b) Shutterstock © Fotomicar ; p29 iStock © Frans Rombout

Library of Congress Cataloging-in-Publication Data

Heneghan, Judith.
Love your dog / by Judith Heneghan.
    p. cm. — (Your perfect pet)
Includes index.
ISBN 978-1-4777-0185-0 (library binding) — ISBN 978-1-4777-0198-0 (pbk.) —
ISBN 978-1-4777-0199-7 (6-pack)
1. Dogs—Juvenile literature. I. Title.
SF426.5.H437 2013
636.7—dc23

                        2012026233

Manufactured in the United States of America

CPSIA Compliance Information: Batch # BW13WM: For Further Information contact Windmill Books, New York, New York at 1-866-478-0556

Contents

A New Puppy

I love our dog Tipper. We chose her because she is so friendly, but there was a lot to think about first. She came to live with us when she was 12 weeks old. Now she is part of our family.

The big question...

Can I get a dog?

Dogs need a warm, safe home, a good diet, a suitable place where they can exercise every day, toys, company, and a lot of care. They are also expensive to take care of. The information in this book will help you decide whether a dog is right for you.

All dogs are different. They have different personalities, too. Do you want a dog that needs lots of exercise, or one that is used to other dogs and enjoys making new friends? Young dogs have lots of energy, while an older dog might be more set in its ways. Thinking about why you want a dog will help you choose the right one.

Furry facts

Newborn puppies have no teeth and can't open their eyes. They need to be with their mothers until they are at least 8 weeks old.

Watch your puppy with its parents and brothers and sisters to see how it behaves. Make sure they are all happy and confident.

Getting Ready

We got everything ready at home before we collected Tipper. I put her bed in a quiet corner of the kitchen. We moved dangerous hazards like electric cables and checked that our garden was safe and secure for her.

The big question...

Should we use a dog crate?

A dog crate must be big enough for your dog to stand up in, turn around, and lie down stretched out. Your dog will need a water bowl, bedding, and toys in there, too. A crate can be useful if you are worried about your dog's safety when you are not watching it for a short time. Never put a dog in a crate to punish it. A crate should be a happy place for your dog!

All dogs need a comfy, dry, clean, and quiet place to sleep. If you buy a special dog bed, choose one that is big enough for your dog to lie stretched out. If you have more than one dog, make sure they each have a bed.

Young puppies need lots of sleep to grow.

Furry facts

Dogs have an excellent sense of smell. When you collect your puppy, ask if you can take one of its toys or blankets home with you. The familiar smell will help your puppy feel safe on the journey home.

Settling In

Tipper whimpered a little on her first night. I think she missed her brothers and sisters. It didn't last long, though. She settled in quickly and the next day she was ready to explore her new home.

The big question...

Can our puppy sleep in my bedroom?

Dogs are quick learners. If you are happy for your dog to sleep in your bedroom, it will soon feel at home there. However, if there are areas where you don't want your dog to go, be clear about this from the start. Don't confuse your dog. Be consistent.

It is the law to make sure your dog wears a name tag with your home contact details on it.

Puppies have baby teeth, just like we do. These baby teeth start to fall out when the puppy is three or four months old. Then they grow their adult teeth. As it grows, your puppy will love to chew. A suitable chew toy is better than your shoes!

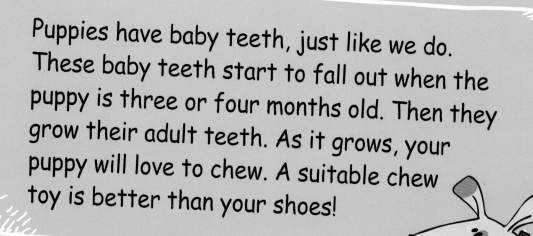

Pet power

Dogs show their feelings in their appearance and behavior. A dog that flattens its ears and drops its tail between its legs may be feeling nervous. A dog that wags its tail and lets its ears move up and forward may be happy and curious.

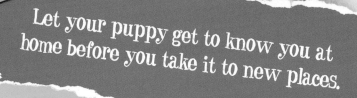

Let your puppy get to know you at home before you take it to new places.

Food and Water

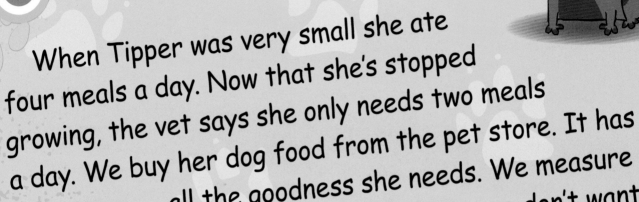

When Tipper was very small she ate four meals a day. Now that she's stopped growing, the vet says she only needs two meals a day. We buy her dog food from the pet store. It has all the goodness she needs. We measure it out carefully because we don't want her to become overweight.

The big question...

Can I give my dog treats?

Most dogs love food, and a few doggie treats are a great way to reward your dog for good behavior. However, try to avoid treats that are full of sugar or fat as these are bad for your dog's teeth and general health.

A few treats are fine as part of a well-balanced diet.

Every dog needs constant access to fresh, clean drinking water. If you go out, always make sure your dog can reach its bowl. Dogs can't tell you when they're thirsty, but they soon become dehydrated and this can be very dangerous.

Furry facts

Some human foods such as chocolate and onions are poisonous for dogs. If your dog has eaten chocolate, call your vet.

Always check the packaging to make sure you are giving your dog the right amount of food for its age and size.

Keeping Clean

Tipper had to learn to go to the bathroom outside. At first she made messes on the kitchen floor, but we kept taking her out onto the grass. Every time she got it right, we praised her. She soon realized that outside was the place to go!

The big question...

How can I get my dog to take a bath?

Some dogs don't like being washed. Bathe your puppy from a young age to make it easier when they are older. Ask your vet for advice about how often to wash your dog and which products to use.

Sometimes dogs get dirty. They might run through the mud, or even roll in something that smells good to them, but smells stinky to us! Use plain water to wash your dog. If you decide to use a dog shampoo, make sure that it won't irritate your dog's eyes or skin and that the smell won't upset your dog.

Pet power

Dogs like to be clean. If you get mad at them for urinating in the wrong place, they may become anxious. The best way to train dogs is to praise and reward them when they go in the right place.

Always take a bag to clear up your dog's waste when you are in a public place like a park.

Vet Check

We took Tipper to the vet just after she came to live with us. She sat on the scale so the vet could check her weight. Then she had a vaccination to stop her from getting ill. She didn't seem to mind too much, but I still gave her lots of praise.

Furry facts

Puppies should not mix with other dogs until they have been vaccinated. This is to protect them from some common diseases that spread from dog to dog.

All dogs need a check-up at least once a year.

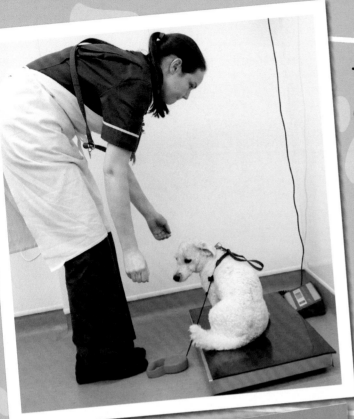

The vet will check your dog's weight, examine its teeth and gums, give it any vaccinations it needs, and advise you on how to protect your dog from worms or fleas. They might also talk to you about microchipping and neutering (see page 26).

The big question...

What is microchipping?

Microchipping is a great way to identify your dog if it is lost or stolen. First, the vet injects a tiny microchip under a dog's skin. Each microchip has its own unique number. Once the chip is in place the dog can't feel it but someone using a scanner can detect it. They can then match the number to the owner's details which are stored in a national database.

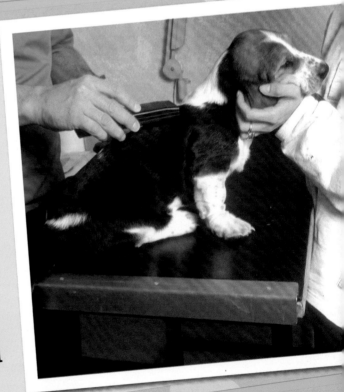

A lost dog that has been microchipped stands a much better chance of being reunited with its owner.

Playtime!

Tipper loves to play. I know when she wants some fun because she nudges me with her nose or fetches her chewy toy and drops it by my feet. Ball games are her favorite. When I play football with my friends, she always joins in.

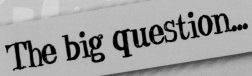

Make sure your dog's toys are safe with no loose parts. They should be the right size for your dog. Avoid anything that might cause your dog to choke.

The big question...

Why does my dog lie down when she sees another dog?

Most dogs love meeting and playing with other dogs. A dog that lies down low when it sees another dog may be feeling a bit nervous, but often it is just showing that it isn't a threat.

Dogs are intelligent animals and playing can help stop them from feeling bored or stressed. Activities like chasing a ball or exploring a cardboard box are fun, but they also help your puppy learn about the world. Play is a great way to build trust and friendship with your dog, too.

Pet power

Have you ever seen a dog do a bow? Dogs often do this to signal that they are feeling playful and they want you to join in. A wagging tail can be another playful signal.

This dog wants to play!

Training Fun

Tipper enjoys learning new things. She has learned to "sit" and "stay" and she comes to me when I call her name. Now I am teaching her a new command. I ask her to "leave" when she brings me her ball. If she drops it, I can throw it for her again!

The best reward is lots of praise and attention.

The big question...

Should I take my dog to a training class?

A training class is a great way to learn how to give commands in a clear and consistent way. They are good training for dog owners! They also introduce your puppy to other dogs which is an important part of their learning experience.

It's a good idea to use a clear hand signal as well as a command word when you are training your dog as this can help it understand.

Training should always be fun for your dog. The best way to train your dog is to reward correct behavior with lots of praise and a treat. Be patient, and don't scold her if she gets it wrong. Just keep trying until she gets it right. Ask an expert if you are still having problems.

Furry facts

Some dogs are trained to work for their owners. Farmers train dogs to round up sheep and cattle. The police train dogs to sniff out explosives or drugs. Other dogs are trained to act as the eyes or ears of blind or deaf owners, helping them cross the road safely or alerting them when the doorbell rings.

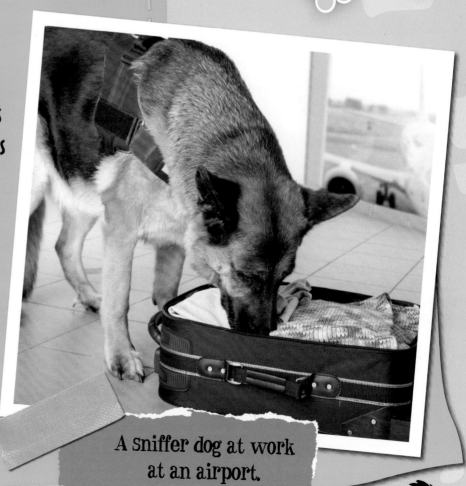

A sniffer dog at work at an airport.

Off for a Walk

Tipper isn't a big dog, but she still needs plenty of exercise. We take her for a walk twice a day. While we are on the pavement, she walks next to me on the leash. When we get to the park, she runs free and sniffs everything, including her other doggy friends!

Introduce your dog to a variety of settings so that it gets used to different sights, sounds, and smells.

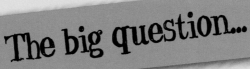

The big question...

How much exercise does my puppy need?

A puppy shouldn't really be going for walks outside the home until it is 12 weeks old. Once your puppy has been vaccinated, start to take it for short walks and build this up gradually. Adult dogs should have the opportunity to run every day.

This dog has been trained to walk without pulling on the leash.

Dogs need lots of exercise. It helps them stay fit and healthy, but it also means they can meet other dogs, visit new places and, most important, sniff all the interesting smells.

Dogs enjoy exploring new places.

Pet power

Dogs use their noses to find out about the world around them. Their sense of smell is thousands of times more sensitive than ours, and their wet noses can accurately identify the direction of each new smell.

Good Grooming

Tipper has thick, wiry hair. I brush her coat every couple of days with a special dog brush. This helps get rid of old hair and leaves her coat looking healthy and glossy. She seems to enjoy it!

Brushing from the head toward the tail helps get rid of old hair. Get your dog used to it from an early age if you can.

Furry facts

Dogs shed their hair throughout the year, constantly replacing it with new hair. However, they may shed greater amounts in the spring and the autumn. This is so that they can grow a fresh summer coat or winter coat to match the changes in temperature.

Insects like fleas and ticks love dogs, because they can bury themselves in their thick hair and feed on their blood. But fleas and ticks will make your dog scratch and feel uncomfortable, and they can pass the insects to humans, too. Ask your vet for advice on how to prevent the arrival of these pests.

Your vet may suggest an anti-flea treatment that you can give your dog at home.

The big question...

Should I clip my dog's nails?

Most dogs don't need to have their nails clipped, because they wear down naturally as they walk. Check your dog's nails regularly to make sure they aren't growing too long. Ask your vet for advice if you are worried.

Going Away

Last year we went on vacation to the beach. Tipper came with us. We made sure we were staying in a place that welcomed dogs and was safe for her. She made the trip extra special.

If you take your dog to the beach, check first to see if dogs are allowed. Make sure your dog can sit in the shade and has access to fresh water.

The big question...

Is it safe to take our dog in the car?

Dogs can get used to traveling by car, but make sure they have enough room to move around and get comfortable. Always take fresh water with you so your dog can have a drink, and stop to let it out at least every hour so it can exercise and go to the bathroom. Without fresh air and fresh water, dogs become seriously ill.

Never leave a dog alone in a car, even on a cloudy day.

24

If you have to leave your dog at home alone for a few hours, make sure it has plenty of fresh water and ask a friend or neighbor to let it run outside. Dogs can get lonely on their own. If your dog has a particular problem, ask a behavior expert for help.

Pet power

Dogs bark to communicate. They may want something or need something. It might be a treat, or a walk, or to warn you that a stranger is approaching. But sometimes dogs bark because they are bored, or because they have been left on their own for too long. A dog never barks for no reason.

Getting Older

Tipper is three years old now. She's not a puppy anymore. She's a bit calmer than she used to be, and she's learned to "leave" and "fetch." She still loves playing with her chew toys, though!

The big question...

What is neutering?

Neutering is the name of an operation to stop your male or female dog from breeding and having puppies. The operation is performed by a vet, and experts recommend it unless you are absolutely sure that if your dog has puppies you can find them all good homes.

Older dogs have different needs. Mature dogs sometimes develop problems with their eyes, their ears, their joints, or their teeth, just like humans do. If you notice any unusual changes in your dog's appearance, general health, or behavior, visit the vet for a check up.

Furry facts

A healthy, well-cared for dog can live for up to 12–14 years, though it depends on the breed. Some dogs are known to have survived into their late twenties!

As dogs get older, their bodies slow down and they may need more rest.

Best Friends

Tipper and I have loads of fun. We play together, go for walks, and she's always happy to see me. She keeps me busy, but she's worth it. She's my best friend.

Happy dogs make loyal, faithful companions.

Pet power

Dogs communicate through their tails. A dog with its tail between its legs may be feeling scared. A high tail shows confidence, and a tail that is straight out means the dog is feeling normal and alert. Dogs generally wag their tails when they are feeling friendly.

Dogs need a warm, safe home, a good diet, a suitable place where they can exercise every day, toys, and loving owners who give them lots of attention.

Furry facts

Dogs are descended from wolves. They have been living alongside humans for thousands of years which makes them the original companion animal and mankind's first pet.

Dogs need lots of care to keep them happy and healthy.

Quiz

How well do you know dogs?
Try this quick quiz to find out!

1. **When is it safe to leave a dog on its own in a car?**
    a. When it's sunny.
    b. Only when the weather's cloudy.
    c. Never.

2. **Which of these foods is poisonous for dogs?**
    a. Apples
    b. Chocolate
    c. Bread

3. **Why would you give your dog a treat?**
    a. Because you want them to be quiet
    b. As a reward for good behavior
    c. Because they ask you for one

4. **How often should you take the dog to vet?**
    a. At least once a year
    b. Never
    c. Once a month

5. **Why is it a good idea to have your dog microchipped?**
    a. So that you always know where to find your dog
    b. Because microchipping helps reunite lost dogs with their owners
    c. Because it saves you from having to train your dog to come when you call its name

6. **What does your dog need on a hot day at the beach?**
    a. Sunscreen
    b. Ice cream
    c. Shade and water

7. **Dogs have wet noses because:**
    a. They get lots of colds
    b. They lick their noses a lot
    c. A wet nose is more sensitive

8. **Dogs are descended from**
    a. Wolves
    b. Foxes
    c. Dinosaurs

Answers

1(c); 2(b); 3(b); 4(a); 5(b); 6(c); 7(c); 8(a)

Glossary

breed (BREED) Type of dog such as Labrador or terrier.

companion (kum-PAN-yun) Friend.

consistent (kun-SIS-tent) Always the same.

contact details (KON-takt dih-TAYLZ) Information that someone can use to get in touch with you, such as an address or telephone number.

database (DAY-tuh-bays) Computerized list.

dehydrated (dee-HY-drayt-ed) A dangerous lack of water.

descended (dih-SEN-did) To come from a particular kind of ancestor.

diet (DY-ut) Food that animals normally eat.

fleas (FLEEZ) Small, jumping, blood-sucking insects.

microchipping (MY-kruh-chip-ing) Injecting a tiny electronic chip under the skin.

neutering (NOO-ter-ing) An operation to stop a dog from breeding and having puppies. Neutering can stop a dog from having health problems in later life and can make it easier to train, too.

panting (PANT-ing) Breathing quickly with the tongue out.

scanner (SKA-ner) A handheld device used to find and read microchips.

soiled (SOYLD) Dirty.

submissive (sub-MIH-siv) The opposite of aggressive.

ticks (TIKS) Blood-sucking insects.

vaccination (vak-suh-NAY-shun) An injection to prevent disease.

worms (WERMZ) Tiny animals that can live in your dog's gut.

Index

Websites

For web resources related to the subject of this book, go to:
www.windmillbooks.com/weblinks
and select this book's title.